Celebrities with ♥ Heart

Oprah Winfrey

Celebrity with Heart

Jen Jones

Enslow Publishers, Inc.
40 Industrial Road
Box 398
Berkeley Heights, NJ 07922
USA
http://www.enslow.com

Library of Congress Cataloging-in-Publication Data

Jones, Jen.
  Oprah Winfrey : celebrity with heart / Jen Jones.
     p. cm. — (Celebrities with heart)
  Summary: "A biography of American media personality Oprah Winfrey"—Provided by
publisher.
  Includes bibliographical references and index.
  ISBN 978-0-7660-3406-8
  1. Winfrey, Oprah—Juvenile literature. 2. Television personalities—United States—
Biography—Juvenile literature. 3. Actors—United States—Biography—Juvenile literature.
I. Title.
  PN1992.4.W56J665 2011
  791.4502'8092—dc22
  [B]
                                   2009023811
ISBN-13: 978-1-59845-206-8 (paperback ed.)

052010 Lake Book Manufacturing, Inc., Melrose Park, IL

Printed in the United States of America

10 9 8 7 6 5 4 3 2 1

To Our Readers: We have done our best to make sure all Internet addresses in this book
were active and appropriate when we went to press. However, the author and publisher
have no control over and assume no liability for the material available on those Internet sites
or on other Web sites they may link to. Any comments or suggestions can be sent by e-mail
to comments@enslow.com or to the address on the back cover.

Every effort has been made to locate all copyright holders of material used in this book.
If any errors or omissions have occurred, corrections will be made in future editions of this book.

♻ Enslow Publishers, Inc., is committed to printing our books on recycled paper. The
paper in every book contains 10% to 30% post-consumer waste (PCW). The cover board
on the outside of each book contains 100% PCW. Our goal is to do our part to help young
people and the environment too!

Illustration Credits: Associated Press, pp. 1, 4, 6, 11, 28, 35, 37, 49, 68, 74, 78, 81, 91,
99, 103, 105; © Buena Vista Pictures/courtesy Everett Collection, p. 44; Kosciusko Tourist
Promotion Council, p. 17; Adam Larkey/© Harpo Productions/courtesy Everett Collection,
p. 64; Metropolitan Government Archives of Nashville and Davidson County, pp. 19, 21,
22; personal collection of Oprah Winfrey, p. 14; Shutterstock, pp. 26, 54; Charles Sykes/Rex
Features/courtesy Everett Collection, p. 31; © Warner Brothers/courtesy Everett Collection,
p. 41.

Cover Illustration: Associated Press (Oprah Winfrey in a brown gown).

Contents

Oprah Winfrey

The Midas Touch

O, what a life! As a highly successful media mogul, philanthropist, and television personality, Oprah Winfrey has become one of the most powerful and admired people on the planet. In fact, Winfrey was second only to Mother Teresa in a 1997 poll about public figures most likely to go to heaven.[1] ("You could really put 'Reverend' in front of her name," one fan gushed at a 2005 appearance in Washington, D.C.[2]) With *The Oprah Winfrey Show* perched firmly atop the ratings heap for more than twenty years and a steadily growing media empire, Winfrey has truly embraced her platform as a means of spreading joy, inspiration, and empowerment for all.

As a by-product of the show's popularity, many viewers have begun to take Winfrey's word as "gospel"—hanging on to her every book, film, and product recommendation. Sales and reputation typically soar after Winfrey endorses something on the air, resulting in what some experts call the "Oprah Factor." In fact, some believe Winfrey to be the most influential woman in the world. *Vanity Fair* once asserted, "Oprah Winfrey arguably has more influence on the culture than any university, president, politician, or religious leader, except perhaps the Pope."[3]

Oprah Winfrey traveled to Durban, South Africa, in 2002 to give thousands of children food, clothes, school supplies, books, and toys on behalf of her charity, the Oprah Winfrey Foundation.

This influence is perhaps best illustrated by her popular on-air book club, which began in 1996. Blending girlfriend gab with literary analysis, Winfrey invited millions of viewers into her virtual living room to talk about books that had her buzzing. For the first six years, the selections focused on modern fiction; after taking a brief hiatus from 2002 to 2003, Winfrey began exploring the classics, such as Steinbeck's *East of Eden*. Winfrey was thrilled to share one of her personal passions with the world: "Books allowed me a new way of seeing myself, helped me to create a vision that has exceeded even my grandest dreams. Opened the door to experiences and connections I never knew existed," Winfrey said in a 1999 acceptance speech for the National Book Award. "The real blessing for us all at the book club is now being able to open that door for somebody else."[4]

Along with introducing viewers to quality stories, Winfrey also propelled numerous authors to unprecedented success. A 2003 *Forbes* story stated that all forty-six of Winfrey's selections to date had been instant best sellers,[5] while *Publishers Weekly* mused that "for debut novels, a nod from Oprah is the only way to real success."[6] *People* also weighed in with the tongue-in-cheek, "A Pulitzer Prize is nice. A Nobel even nicer. But to hit the literary jackpot these days, what an author wants is an Oprah."[7]

And authors were just as effusive in their praise: Melinda Haynes credited Winfrey with her move from a trailer into a five-bedroom house as "the house that Oprah built." Janet Fitch, whose novel *White Oleander* was made into a movie after Winfrey's selection, was just as grateful: "I feel like the old Chinese belief—the one where when somebody saves your life, you belong to that person forever. I really feel that way about Oprah."[8]

Winfrey's reputation as a tastemaker does not stop at books. Her "What's the Buzz?" segments explore the hottest movies, music, and other pieces of pop culture, and audiences are often eager to follow Winfrey's picks. From Oscar to Emmy to Grammy winners, celebrities are happy to talk with Winfrey and promote their latest projects. Winfrey has also helped up-and-coming musical talent reach the tipping point, boosting sales of such rising stars as Leona Lewis, Josh Groban, and Robin Thicke.

Some followers are influenced to the extreme—case in point being thirty-five-year-old Robyn Okrant, who devoted an entire year of her life to following Winfrey's advice. Throughout 2008, Okrant documented her experiences on a blog titled "Living Oprah." From coloring her hair to seeing Celine Dion in concert at Winfrey's urging, Okrant carried out her mission with vigor. Wrote Okrant, "I am performing an experiment: for one year, I will live as Oprah advises on her television show, on her website, and in the pages of her magazines. . . . I wonder, will I truly find bliss if I commit wholeheartedly to her lifestyle suggestions?"[9] At the end of her journey, Okrant shared the many lessons she had learned about herself and what she took away from it: "I don't know about this whole 'Best Life' thing. I'm living my ONLY life. I am reminded daily that I must be grateful for every second of it."[10]

So why do Oprah Winfrey's fans believe in her so strongly? Simply put, Winfrey's down-to-earth "one of us" approach has earned the widespread trust of her viewership. Her choice of Chaka Khan's "I'm Every Woman" as the show's theme song spoke volumes about Winfrey's ability to relate to just about anyone. From fat to thin, rags to riches, abused to empowered, Winfrey's rich and varied life experiences are reflected in the millions of fans she reaches daily. And even when she has not experienced something personally, Winfrey shows extreme interest and compassion for her guests. "What she lacks in journalistic toughness, she makes up for in plainspoken curiosity, robust humor and, above all, empathy," read a 1988 *Time* article. "Guests with sad stories to tell are apt to rouse a tear in Oprah's eye.... They, in turn, often find themselves revealing things they would not imagine telling anyone, much less a national TV audience."[11]

Winfrey's intimate interactions also include sharing access to lifestyle experts much the same way friends would trade referrals for doctors or hairstylists. Inside Oprah Winfrey's world are spiritual gurus, money wizards, trained psychologists, interior designers, and all types of other experts—all ready and willing to help viewers better their lives. A typical day on Winfrey's show might include a visit from Dr. Mehmet Oz giving anti-aging secrets or life coach Martha Beck sharing ways to de-stress. For many of these experts, appearing on Winfrey's show has propelled their businesses and books to massive success.

Perhaps the best example of an *Oprah* expert benefiting from the "Oprah factor" is Dr. Phil McGraw—best known to audiences as simply "Dr. Phil." In 1998, McGraw started appearing on Winfrey's show as a recurring "life strategy and relationship expert." Audiences were intrigued by his frank, brutally honest brand of psychology, as was Winfrey. "He has the foresight and skill to look at any situation, cut through the psychobabble, and call it as he sees it—and he's usually right," Winfrey wrote on her Web site.[12] In September 2002, McGraw signed on with Winfrey's Harpo Productions to head his own daytime talk show. The show was an instant hit, and its launch boasted the highest ratings for a new talk show since Winfrey's own start in 1986.[13]

McGraw was publicly grateful for Winfrey's role in launching him to stardom, thanking her profusely in his book *Life Strategies:* "I thank Oprah for awakening in me the desire and inspiring in me the commitment to reach out and share with others that which I believe with such clarity and passion," he wrote. "Without Oprah, there would be no *Life Strategies,* which for me would be a personal tragedy. . . . I thank Oprah for caring, for doing it right, and for sharing her platform with me."[14]

Oprah Winfrey celebrates outside the courthouse in Amarillo, Texas, February 26, 1998, after the jury ruled in her favor in the beef defamation trial.

Another Oprah Winfrey expert-turned-Harpo host is Food Network star Rachael Ray. Blending Ray's trademark food segments with lighthearted lifestyle topics, the peppy chef's daytime talk show hit the airwaves in 2006. True to form, Winfrey's blessing gave the show good opening karma—posting the highest ratings for a talk show launch since Dr. Phil.[15] (Winfrey then appeared as a guest on the show's second day on the air.)

Yet Winfrey's endorsement has not always gone as planned. In April 1996, Winfrey ignited a controversy during an episode titled "Dangerous Foods." During a segment about mad cow disease, Winfrey exclaimed, "It has just stopped me cold from eating another burger!"[16] Her brief, innocent statement had lasting consequences— the cattle industry lost an estimated $87.6 million in a matter of weeks as a result of consumers forgoing beef. In response, cattle producers withdrew six hundred thousand dollars in advertising from Winfrey's network and filed a lawsuit in 1997.[17]

The *Texas Beef Group vs. Oprah Winfrey* trial took place in Amarillo, Texas, considered by many to be "cattle country." A media frenzy surrounded the trial, with one Texan reporter dubbing the trial "Beauty and the Beef."[18] The judge eventually ruled that Winfrey was not responsible for paying any damages, and Winfrey emerged from the courtroom with her fists raised in victory.[19]

It is clear that when Oprah Winfrey talks, people listen. Her fans have followed every step of her self-made journey, forming a great deal of respect for their favorite television personality. "This is a woman that came from nothing to rise up to be the most powerful woman, I think, in the world," FOX News host Bill O'Reilly has said. "I mean, she has a loyal following; she has credibility; she has talent; and she's done it on her own to become fabulously wealthy and fabulously powerful."[20]

Trials and Triumphs

Born on January 29, 1954, Oprah Gail[1] Winfrey was originally named "Orpah" after a biblical character in the Book of Ruth. Accounts differ of how her name actually morphed into "Oprah." Some reports state that a nurse misspelled her given name on the birth certificate, while still others say that friends and family often mispronounced and misspelled her name and it stuck permanently. In any case—regardless of how it was truly created—"Oprah" was destined to become one of the most recognizable names in recent history.

At the time of Oprah's birth, her parents were unmarried; in fact, at one point, Oprah called their relationship a "one-day fling under an oak tree."[2] Her mother, Vernita Lee, was eighteen years old, while her father, Vernon Winfrey, was twenty. It was decided that until Vernita could properly support a child on her own, Oprah would be raised by her maternal grandparents, Hattie Mae and Earless Lee, on their farm in Kosciusko, Mississippi.

Even at a young age, Oprah started to show signs of the personality traits that would make her famous. A precocious child, Oprah displayed a knack for connecting

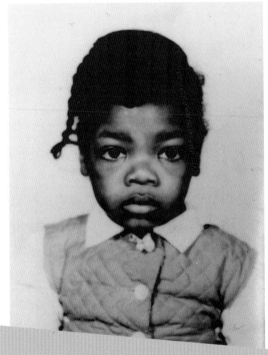

From a very early age, Oprah showed a love for reading and communicating with others.

with others and making her opinions known. (She later told CNN, "People would say to my grandmother, 'Hattie Mae, this child sure can talk!'"[3]) Oprah also learned how to read and recite Bible verses at a very young age—foreshadowing the love of books that would later come into play on her television show. According to Oprah, "Books were my pass to personal freedom. I learned to read at age three, and soon discovered there was a whole world to conquer that went beyond our farm in Mississippi."[4]

Life on the farm was a bonding experience for Oprah and her grandmother. Oprah often helped Hattie Mae with chores, such as feeding the chickens, hanging laundry, making soap, or bringing buckets of water into the house, which had no indoor plumbing. Some of Oprah's most treasured memories include attending Faith United Baptist Church on Sundays and watching her grandmother cook generous Southern-style dinners. While Hattie Mae was a strict yet strong positive influence, Oprah's grandfather Earless Lee was not: "[He was] always a dark presence," Oprah told the *New York Times Magazine* in 1989. "I remember him always throwing things at me or trying to shoo me away with his cane. I lived in absolute terror."[5]

Living in near poverty was also difficult. Because the house had no indoor plumbing, Oprah was only able to bathe once a week.[6] Her only doll was made from a dried corncob, and her clothes were made of potato sacks—prompting other kids to nickname her "Sack Girl."[7] Hattie

Mae could afford to purchase Oprah just two pairs of shoes per year, which Oprah wore only to church.[8] Yet despite the lack of material things, Hattie Mae provided Oprah with more valuable gifts. "I am what I am because of my grandmother," Oprah has said. "My strength. My sense of reasoning. Everything. All that was set by the time I was six."[9]

In 1960, Oprah left her grandmother's care and moved to Milwaukee to live with her mother. Even though she had left the farm, conditions were still difficult: Vernita lived in the inner city in a space so tiny that Oprah had to sleep in the foyer. In order to get by, Vernita worked long hours as a housemaid—leaving little time to spend with her daughter. "She was just trying to survive," Winfrey remembered. "Her way of showing love to me was getting out and going to work every day, putting clothes on my back and having food on the table. At that time, I didn't understand it."[10]

Oprah's times in Milwaukee were trying. At the age of nine, Oprah was staying at her uncle's house overnight when her nineteen-year-old male cousin raped her. "As I trembled and cried, he took me for an ice cream and convinced me not to tell—and for 12 years I didn't," Winfrey later wrote in *O* magazine. "When you are sexually violated, it's not the physical act that destroys you. It's the weight of the secret you feel you have to keep, the person you have to become so no one will discover what you're hiding."[11] Unfortunately, the abuse did not stop there—in the years to come, Oprah also suffered sexual abuse from other family friends and relatives.

In her early teen years, Oprah started exhibiting bad behavior: skipping school, running away, and stealing money from her mother. Oprah also experimented with promiscuity,[12] later attributing that behavior to the cycle of abuse she had endured. At the age of fourteen, she became pregnant—a fact that was not disclosed publicly until 1990, when her half sister betrayed her by selling the information to the *National Enquirer.* Young Oprah was

Now the Buffalo Community Center, this was the church Oprah attended with her grandmother in Kosciusko, Mississippi.

so ashamed about the pregnancy that she tried to hide it "until my swollen ankles and belly gave it away. The baby died in the hospital weeks later," Winfrey wrote in *O* magazine.[13]

While pregnant, Oprah once again relocated to Nashville, Tennessee, to live with her father, Vernon, and his wife, Zelma. She had stayed with them briefly during her fourth-grade year, and Vernita felt it would be best for Oprah to return permanently. A barber and grocery store owner, Vernon was well established and better able to provide a stable home environment. He also believed in strong discipline and could help Oprah's life get back on track. "When my father took me, it changed the course of my life," Winfrey has said. "He saved me.... I was definitely headed for a career as a juvenile delinquent."[14]

Oprah enrolled at Nashville East High School, where she was voted "Most Popular Girl"[15] and became an honors student. Vernon and Zelma were strict, enforcing an early curfew and assigning Oprah books to read each week. Vernon brought Oprah to church with him every Sunday—where she would read sermons by James Weldon Johnson to the congregation. "I've been an orator, basically, all of my life," Winfrey said in an interview with the Academy of Achievement. "Since I was three and a half, I've been coming up in the church speaking."[16]

Oprah's oratory skills would soon get her noticed in a major way. As a member of her high school's speech and debate team, Oprah earned second place in a national contest for dramatic interpretation.[17] For her prize, she was awarded a full scholarship to Tennessee State University. Around the same time, Oprah was one of two students picked to represent Tennessee at the White House Conference on Youth. As the result of a radio interview she did about the conference, Oprah was also selected to

Oprah moved to Nashville, Tennessee, to live with her father, Vernon Winfrey, who could provide a better living environment for her. She credits her father with saving her from a life of delinquency.

compete in the 1971 "Miss Fire Prevention" pageant in Nashville.

As the only African-American girl in the contest, Oprah was convinced that she had no chance of winning. She felt relaxed and decided to view the pageant as a fun experience. "There was a question about what I would like to do with my life, my career. Well, everybody wanted to be a nurse, or a teacher, and I made this big speech about broadcast journalism—mainly because I had seen Barbara Walters that morning on *The Today Show*," Winfrey recalled. "I thought, 'Well, what can I be? I can't be a nurse, can't be a teacher because that's what they were.' So I said I wanted to be a broadcast journalist because I believed in the truth. I was interested in proclaiming the truth to the world and all. And I won the contest."[18]

Seventeen-year-old Oprah was soon to get her wish: WVOL, the radio station that had sponsored the pageant, offered her an after-school job reading news on the air. She continued working at WVOL as a student at Tennessee State University as well as her involvement with the pageant scene. (After winning the title of Miss Black Tennessee, Oprah competed in Miss Black America in 1972.) Soon Oprah started to receive offers to do television news, but at first she was hesitant: "I turned them down three times. The third time, I [approached my] college professor. I said, 'They keep calling me to be on television. And I know if I do television, I'll never finish school.' So he said, 'Don't you know that's why people go to school? So that somebody can keep calling them, you nit-wit!'"[19]

During her sophomore year, Oprah Winfrey accepted a job at WLAC-TV and became the first African-American female news anchor in Nashville.[20] Just nineteen years old, Winfrey found it difficult to juggle school, work, and social obligations. A typical day

Oprah's senior portrait from Nashville East High School. She did very well both academically and socially. Among her numerous accomplishments were winning academic honors and being elected vice-president of the student council.

In 1971, Oprah waves during her victory ride as Nashville's first African-American Miss Fire Prevention.

included classes from 8 A.M. to 2 P.M., work from 2 P.M. to 10 P.M., and studying until well after midnight. Winfrey was asked to join a sorority, but her busy schedule prevented her from doing so. "I didn't have the time to be a part of all the other college activities, or a part of that whole lifestyle," Winfrey remembered. "It was very difficult for me socially—really one of the worst times of my life, because I was trying to fit in at school, and be a part of that culture, but also trying to build a career in television."[21]

In 1975, Winfrey's graduating class marched without her, as she was short one necessary credit—much to her father's dismay. "My father, from that time on and for years after, was always on my case because I did not graduate," Winfrey later said in a commencement speech at Stanford University. "He'd say, 'Oprah Gail . . . I don't know what you're gonna do without that degree.'" (In 1987, Winfrey finally fulfilled her father's wish. She received her degree from Tennessee State University when she returned to finish her coursework and address that year's graduating class.)[22]

At age twenty-two, Winfrey was offered a job anchoring the six-o'-clock news in Baltimore—a much bigger market than Nashville. Though she remembered the opportunity as "the biggest deal in the world at the time,"[23] the job was stressful and challenging. Executives at the station wanted Winfrey to change her name to "Suzie" and to change her appearance. They also disliked Winfrey's tendency to react emotionally to the news, often laughing or crying instead of reporting in a straightforward manner. She was fired after eight months, but not before learning an important lesson: "It took me messing up on the air, during a live newscast. I was doing a list of foreign countries . . . and I called Canada 'Ca-NAD-a.' I got so tickled . . . and then I started laughing," remembered Winfrey. "For me, the beginning of realizing that, 'Oh, you can laugh at yourself and you can make a mistake and it's not the end of the world.'"[24]

The station found Winfrey a more suitable home for her candid on-air style at WJZ-TV cohosting a one-hour local talk show, *People Are Talking*. A billboard campaign promoting Winfrey as the new host bore the simple slogan, "What's an Oprah?"[25] Baltimore appeared eager to find out the answer: the show was a smash hit, earning even higher ratings than the popular *Phil Donahue Show*.[26] During this time, Winfrey also hosted a game show for the same station called *Dialing for Dollars*. Winfrey remembered her experience on *People Are Talking* as the first time she realized her calling: "The minute the first show was over, I thought, 'Thank God, I've found what I was meant to do,'" Winfrey has said. "It's like breathing to me."[27]

Small-Screen Queen

Though Winfrey had found her calling in Baltimore, Chicago was the place where she ultimately embraced her destiny. Upon moving to the Windy City in 1983, Winfrey immediately felt a sense of excitement about the possibilities it held: "My first day in Chicago ... I set foot in this city, and just walking down the street, it was like roots, like the motherland. I knew I belonged here."[1]

Winfrey's motivation for moving was an offer to host *AM Chicago,* a morning talk show in danger of cancellation. Debra DiMaio, a former assistant producer on Baltimore's *People Are Talking,* had moved to Chicago to produce the show, and recommended Winfrey to assume the vacant hosting position. Executive producer Dennis Swanson remembered the first time DiMaio showed him Winfrey's audition tape: "I had looked at tapes for years, but never had I seen anything like Oprah. She is a unique personality. So up. So effervescent. So television. So spontaneous and unrehearsed. She was not like anyone else on the tube."[2]

Not surprisingly, Winfrey's involvement helped turn the show's fate around quickly. Within a month, the show surpassed *Donahue* to take Chicago's number-one spot.[3]

Winfrey moved to Chicago, Illinois, to host *AM Chicago* and save it from cancellation. Upon arriving, she felt the city was her true home.

It appeared audiences were ready for a change from Phil Donahue's somber, journalistic approach—and Winfrey's engaging, compassionate way was just the remedy. "Unlike Donahue, Winfrey opens up to the audience, talking to the camera as one would to a friend," wrote Jennifer Harris and Elwood Watson in *The Oprah Phenomenon*.[4] Georgetown professor Deborah Tannen weighed in as well, calling Donahue's style "report talk" versus Oprah's "rapport talk."[5]

Less than a year later, the show was expanded to one hour and its name changed to *The Oprah Winfrey Show*. In light of the show's runaway success, syndication company King World approached Winfrey with an opportunity to bring her show to a national audience. Not sure how to handle the offer, Winfrey approached local movie critic Roger Ebert for advice. "I don't know what to do," Winfrey told Ebert. "The problem with syndication is that if your show isn't successful, you're off the air in three months. The ABC stations own themselves, so they can keep you on. Which way do you think I should go?"[6] As a syndicated television star, Ebert knew the answer—go for it!

In September 1986, Winfrey did just that—making her national debut via syndication. She had assembled a dream team of trusted colleagues, with long-time associate Debra DiMaio acting as executive producer. To celebrate the show's new status, Oprah took a Thanksgiving trip with

Vernon and Zelma Winfrey back to Kosciusko, Mississippi, to share the occasion with family and friends.[7]

Though many talk shows take time to gain momentum, *The Oprah Winfrey Show* was a hit right out of the gate. At the 1987 Daytime Emmys, the show took home prestigious awards for Outstanding Host, Outstanding Talk/Service Show, and Outstanding Direction. For his part, Donahue was very gracious about the new queen in town: "One of the biggest moments of my life came right then," Oprah Winfrey told the *New York Times* in 1988. "After I thanked [Donahue in my speech], he came up to

Winfrey holds up one of the three Emmy awards her show won in 1987.

my table and he kissed me and that's when I knew that [the rivalry] was all media-contrived and he didn't hate me at all! He told me: 'You deserve it, you deserve it, you deserve it.'"[8]

The year 1987 was big for Winfrey not only professionally but also personally. While hitting the fundraiser and party circuit in Chicago, Winfrey had taken notice several times of an intriguing man by the name of Stedman Graham. A model and former basketball player, Graham was also the founder of AAD (Athletes Against Drugs), a nonprofit organization devoted to helping athletes make healthy choices. Though Graham eventually became Winfrey's treasured life partner, she almost did not end up with him. When Graham first asked her out, Winfrey turned him down for fear that he was more enthralled by her fame than by her.[9] Winfrey's employees were not too keen on the idea either: "They figured if he looked like [a model], he either had to be a jerk or want something," Winfrey told *People*.[10]

Yet Graham's persistence paid off—and once he finally convinced her to go on a date, the two were inseparable. Winfrey quickly learned she had been wrong in her initial opinion about Graham. "He's kind and supportive," she said several months into the relationship. "Lots of people want to ride with you in the limo. But you want someone who'll help you catch the bus."[11]

Winfrey would soon become even more grateful for the support of those like Stedman—for in 1988, she undertook another considerable venture: starting her own production company. Winfrey's formula for naming the company was simple: spelling her own name backward. Based in Chicago, Harpo Productions would give Winfrey more control over her career and ownership of her show. It also marked a career milestone, as Winfrey was only the third woman in American history to head her own studio (the others being Lucille Ball and Mary Pickford).

To house Harpo, Winfrey purchased an old hockey rink on Chicago's West Loop neighborhood and converted it into a production facility. At eighty-eight thousand square feet, Harpo's home was quite a sight to behold—housing a staff gym, movie screening room, and in-house spa along with the offices and TV studio.[12,13] Once established inside the studio, Winfrey moved from a live-only format to pretaping some shows. Suddenly, Winfrey had more power over not only her schedule but also her show's subject matter and her own personal stake in it. "If I lost control of the business, I'd lose myself—or at least the ability to be myself. Owning myself is a way to be myself," Winfrey later said.[14]

Winfrey's swift skyrocketing to success did not go unnoticed. As a fitting follow-up to 1987's slew of Daytime Emmy wins, *The Oprah Winfrey Show* continued its winning streak with Best Talk/Service Show awards in

1988 and 1989. In June 1988, the avalanche of accolades continued as Winfrey was awarded the International Radio and Television Society's Broadcaster of the Year Award. Not only was Winfrey the youngest person to receive the IRTS honor in its twenty-five years of existence, but she was also only the fifth woman ever to do so.

Though Winfrey made a huge splash with audiences in the 1980s, the 1990s marked the decade within which her

Stedman Graham has been by Winfrey's side since 1987.

show truly hit its stride. Moving away from tabloid-style stories, Winfrey chose to feature topical explorations of spirituality, health, literature, and women's issues. Looking back, Winfrey was able to pinpoint the exact moment she felt the need for positive change; it was during a live show taping in 1989 in which a cheating husband confessed to his wife that his mistress was pregnant.

"The expression on her face—it pains me to think of it—I looked at her and felt horrible for myself and for her. So I turned to her and said, 'I'm really sorry you had to be put in this position and you had to hear this on television. This never should have happened,'" Winfrey told *Entertainment Weekly*. "I can't say we never did another show with conflict, but that's when I first thought about it."[15]

As part of the overhaul, Winfrey also began to feature A-list celebrities and, in 1993, landed a ninety-minute prime-time interview with the famously reclusive Michael Jackson. As it had been fourteen years since Jackson's last televised interview,[16] viewers were eager to hear what he had to say. More than 100 million tuned in, making it one of the most watched events in television history. On the show, Jackson opened up to Winfrey: "I am one of the loneliest people on this earth," he told her. "I cry sometimes because it hurts. It does. To be honest, I guess you could say it hurts to be me."[17]

Major changes started to take place around 1994, coinciding with Winfrey's fortieth birthday and the departure of executive producer Debra DiMaio. Though Winfrey still wanted to provide a forum for people who had been abused or wronged, she longed for the show to take a more proactive, less "playing the victim" approach. As her big birthday loomed near, Winfrey dove into New Age philosophy and the idea of taking responsibility for your life—and it reflected in the show's new direction. "[Oprah] abandoned the shock format and made spiritual uplift, individual will, personal responsibility, and grand cosmic design the guiding principles of her shows," wrote Jennifer Harris and Elwood Watson in *The Oprah Phenomenon.*[18]

Whereas in the past many of the show's topics had some element of shock value, the new *Oprah Winfrey Show* empowered viewers to change their lives. Topics ranged from "Finding Your Authentic Self" to "Design Your Dream" to "Powerful Words: How to Apologize."[19] Winfrey also assembled a team of experts to provide viewers more in-depth knowledge in various areas: relationship expert John Gray (*Men Are From Mars, Women Are From Venus*), psychologist Dr. Phil, personal finance guru Suze Orman, and motivational speaker Iyanla Vanzant among others. These experts became popular television personalities and were featured regularly on Winfrey's show.

In September 1996, Winfrey introduced a new segment that quickly became a nationwide craze: "Oprah's Book Club." Her first selection was Jacquelyn Mitchard's

Deep End of the Ocean, about a family that reunites with their kidnapped son. "This is one of my all-time favorite moments I'm having on television right now," Winfrey shared excitedly with her viewers. "You are witnessing it—mainly because I love books."[20] Winfrey's influence was immediately evident—the publisher had only printed sixty-eight thousand copies of the book upon its June 1996 release, yet several months after the show, more than 1 million copies reached the shelves.[21]

Toni Morrison, the second author selected, was perplexed but intrigued by this new phenomenon: "I'd never heard of such a thing, and when someone called, all excited, with the news, all I could think was, 'Who's going to buy a book because of Oprah?'"

It turns out Morrison's skepticism was unfounded. After the show, 1 million copies of her book *Song of Solomon* sold, and sales of her other books jumped by 25 percent. Winfrey's subsequent selections followed suit. In March 1999, six of the top fifteen national best sellers were Oprah Book Club selections.[23] At one point, the American Library Association even honored Winfrey for "single-handedly expanding the size of the reading public."[24]

Though at first the book club was only a small part of the show, it eventually grew to be its own hour-long topic. With audiences full of viewers who had read the book, shows featured an author interview and a pretaped segment of Winfrey's small group discussion with five lucky readers. The small group was typically filmed at a dinner party with Winfrey and the author; to win the slots, readers sent in letters about how the book had personally affected or related to their lives. "The best thing about [the book club] is the thousands of letters from people who hadn't picked up a book in 20 years," Winfrey told *Entertainment Weekly* in 1996. "Some literally made me weep."[25]

Winfrey hosts a 2008 episode of "Oprah's Book Club." Many unknown authors have become famous because their books were featured on Winfrey's show.

Yet not everyone was in favor of Winfrey's pet project. Many literary enthusiasts felt that the book club commercialized treasured classics, while critics asserted that viewers blindly followed Winfrey's recommendations without forming valid opinions of their own. "Oprah's critics . . . bemoan the fact that authors of merit struggle to find an audience while Oprah-approved ones gain seemingly effortless public acclaim," wrote Mary Elizabeth Williams in a 1999 piece for Salon.com.[26] In 2001, author Jonathan Franzen complained to numerous media outlets when his book *The Corrections* was selected, and Winfrey subsequently canceled his invitation to appear on the show, saying it was "never her intention to make anyone uncomfortable or cause anyone conflict."[27] However, most authors were in Winfrey's corner; fellow book club author Chris Bohjalian went on record to say that he was "appalled [by Franzen's actions] as a reader who appreciates the incredible amount that Oprah Winfrey has done for books."[28]

The book club was not the only *Oprah* element that got people talking. Over the years, many big-ticket moments have made headlines. In 1988, Winfrey celebrated her sixty-seven-pound weight loss on the air with a flourish. Wearing size ten Calvin Klein jeans,[29] Winfrey gleefully wheeled out a wagon carrying sixty-seven pounds of actual fat! Spring 2005 marked another buzz worthy moment when an overly energetic Tom Cruise burst onto Winfrey's stage to proclaim his obsession with future wife Katie Holmes—much to the surprise of a bewildered Winfrey.

Though moments like those made pop-culture history, many of the episodes that stand out most for Winfrey have been the heartwarming "bring out the Kleenex" moments. On a countdown of her top twenty favorite shows, Winfrey cited a 1998 episode in which a dying mother's video diaries were shared and a 2004 episode about a man whose family died from carbon monoxide fumes. Also among Winfrey's favorites were surprise appearances by her own former fourth grade teacher, Mrs. Duncan, and her celebrity idol, Mary Tyler Moore.[30] Having been on the air for more than twenty years, Winfrey had hundreds of watercooler moments and memories to choose from—and there are sure to be many more before the small-screen queen completes her reign.

In 1988, Winfrey lost sixty-seven pounds and showed off her new slim body wearing size ten jeans.

Renaissance Woman

Alongside her throne as the queen of talk television, Oprah Winfrey also has had an extremely successful acting and producing career. While her talk show sheds the spotlight on real people's stories, this facet of her career allows Winfrey to make a difference by bringing to life what she considers to be important fictional stories.

Though most actresses do not receive Academy Award nominations for their first major roles, Winfrey rarely follows typical form. In 1985, Winfrey made her acting debut in Steven Spielberg's film adaptation of Alice Walker's novel *The Color Purple*. A Pulitzer Prize winner, the book explores the lives of black females in the

South in the 1930s. The job was extremely meaningful for Winfrey, who had strongly identified with the book since her childhood—especially its themes surrounding abuse. "I read the first page of *The Color Purple,* put the book down, and wept," Winfrey remembered. "I could not believe that someone had put this in writing. It was unbelievable."[1]

Winfrey played Sofia, a role that seemed almost tailor-made for her. (In the story, Sofia is even married to a man named Harpo!) A strong, resilient woman, Sofia defiantly rejects the limitations placed on black women of her time—even in the face of abuse and imprisonment. Upon first hearing of the movie project, Winfrey believed that she was meant to portray Sofia. She felt compelled to play the part—even with no previous experience. "I'd never acted in my life, but I felt so intensely that I had to be part of that movie," said Winfrey, who was approached for the job by producer Quincy Jones after he spotted her on television.[2] "I wanted it more than anything in the world, and would have done anything to do it."[3] In a televised interview with Barbara Walters, Winfrey shared that the content of one particular scene had struck a deep emotional chord within her.[4] In the scene, Sofia angrily confronts the main character Celie in a cornfield with these words: "All my life, I had to fight. I had to fight my daddy, I had to fight my uncles, I had to fight my brothers . . . but I ain't never thought I had to fight in my own house." Winfrey recalled nailing the scene in one try because it conjured such vivid memories of her own traumatic childhood experiences.

"[The scene] was the essence, I thought, of my life, and very liberating to live it through Sofia," Winfrey once said. "Because what she is saying is, 'I fought people all my life, and I'm not going to fight in my own house anymore . . . I'm going to have what I deserve.'"[5]

Winfrey received high praise and honors for her heartfelt portrayal of Sofia, including both Academy Award and Golden Globe nominations. Attending the Academy Awards was a huge thrill for Winfrey, who had dreamt of doing so ever since watching Sidney Poitier win for *Lilies in the Field* when she was just ten years old. "[At that time], I thought to myself, 'I'm going to be there!'" Winfrey told Barbara Walters. "It makes me want to cry because that was the first time I thought, 'I can do that.'"[6] Winfrey celebrated the accomplishment in style, wearing a beaded gold and ivory gown to the ceremony—along with a ten-thousand-dollar fur coat dyed purple in honor of the movie.[7]

Along with allowing her to realize a lifelong dream, Winfrey also credits this time in her life with the motivation for her to form Harpo Studios. Throughout shooting *The Color Purple,* Winfrey was under a strict contract that did not allow ample time for other projects. "I was begging for time because I realized that what we were doing was something very special," Winfrey has said. "So the studio

Oprah Winfrey plays Sofia in the 1985 film adaptation of *The Color Purple*. Winfrey shared many hardships with her character, including abuse and poverty.

came about as a result of me wanting more time and creativity and control for myself."[8] From Winfrey's point of view, the creation of Harpo would enable her to not only take on more acting roles, but also to develop and to produce personally relevant projects.

Indeed, more film opportunities followed in the years to come—many that explored central figures, themes, and events in black history. Her first acting role after *The Color Purple* was in the 1986 feature film *Native Son,* based on a novel by Richard Wright about a young African-American male living in the ghetto on Chicago's South Side. Through Harpo, Winfrey then went on to produce and star in numerous television miniseries, including 1989's *The Women of Brewster Place* and 1997's TV movie *When Women Had Wings.* In 1990, Winfrey got the chance to pay tribute to longtime friend and *Color Purple* producer Quincy Jones with a documentary about his life and impact titled *Listen Up: The Lives of Quincy Jones.*

When Winfrey's Book Club caught on in the mid-1990s, the phenomenon reflected itself in her film projects. Titled "Oprah Winfrey Presents," Harpo Films created a series of made-for-television movies that were often based on popular classic and contemporary literature. As testament to the lure of Winfrey's involvement, major stars, such as Academy Award winners Halle Berry, Jack Lemmon, and Eller Burstyn and Emmy winners Michael Imperioli (*The Sopranos*) and Hank Azaria (*The Simpsons*), signed on to star in the projects. Among the books adapted were Zora Neale Hurston's *Their Eyes Were Watching God* and Mitch Albom's *Tuesdays With Morrie,* which drew an impressive 22.5 million viewers.[9]

Yet possibly the most powerful book-to-film adaptation for Winfrey was her producing and starring turn in 1998's *Beloved.* Based on Toni Morrison's Pulitzer Prize-winning novel, *Beloved* tells the tale of a nineteenth-century slave named Sethe. Long fascinated with stories about slavery, Winfrey had first read *Beloved* upon its release in 1987 and

Though Winfrey is known for socially conscious projects, she is not afraid to have a little fun with her acting career. Winfrey has lent her voice to many animated films, giving life to such characters as Gussy the Goose in 2006's *Charlotte's Web*, Judge Bumbleton in 2007's *Bee Movie*, and Eudora in 2009's *The Princess and the Frog.* Yet Winfrey's most famous cameo was on the sitcom *Ellen*, on which Winfrey played a therapist to whom Ellen DeGeneres comes out of the closet. On the show, DeGeneres's character joked, "No one gives you a cake that says, 'Congratulations! You're a lesbian!'" Yet that is exactly what Winfrey did after the show taping—present the real-life Ellen with a cake bearing those words. Indeed, Winfrey makes life sweet for all those around her.

was immediately captivated. The same night she finished the book, she called author Toni Morrison to discuss adapting it into a feature film.[10] Though it was a tough sell, Winfrey eventually convinced Morrison: "She said, and this is kind of charming, 'I am going in my pocketbook and writing a check.' I wasn't talking to a studio or a lawyer but to another human being," Morrison told *Time*. "It reminded me of

Winfrey and Danny Glover star in 1998's *Beloved*.

myself: a single black woman who said, 'Well, I'm doing this. It's going to be hard for me, but that's beside the point.' This was a big project and, for her, a big deal. And she was deadly serious about every aspect of it."[11]

Committed to embodying the experience, Winfrey undertook an off-camera simulation of slavehood in preparation for the role. Her field research included dressing in slave clothing, walking blindfolded down a long country road to a plantation, and journeying through the woods to experience what slave escapes were like.[12] For her part, Morrison was continually impressed with Winfrey's dedication: "As soon as I saw her, I smiled to myself because I did not think of [Oprah as a] brand name. She looked like Sethe. She inhabited the role."[13]

For Winfrey, who had long treasured the book, it was important that the details of the book be meticulously translated to screen. She worked closely with director Jonathan Demme to ensure that the dialogue, wardrobe, and plot stayed true to the original.[14] Having collected slave artifacts from various auctions, Winfrey kept her findings on set—often dedicating scenes to specific slaves by lighting a candle and saying a prayer beforehand. It was clear that the opportunity to chronicle such an important turning point in black history was immense for Winfrey.

"I always thought I knew my black history, the essence of my roots," Winfrey told *Time*. "For years, I have talked about my ancestors being the bridge that I crossed over on—that the reason Oprah Winfrey can exist is because Sojourner Truth did, because Fannie Lou Hammer did, and because Ida B. Wells did. But I have gone from an awareness to a knowing. . . . I now have a sense of what slavery felt like instead of what it looked like."[15]

While *Beloved* was a personal triumph and well received by many critics, audiences did not embrace the movie as hoped. Though the movie cost approximately $80 million to make, it brought in just $22.8 million at the box office domestically.[16] Some members of the press speculated that audiences had a difficult time seeing their beloved talk show host suffering in such a role. Yet Winfrey was still extremely proud of the work created, and, to this day, a painting depicting Winfrey as Sethe hangs in the lobby at Harpo Studios.[17]

Although Winfrey does not currently have any new acting roles in the pipeline, she continues to maintain her appreciation for the art form and the possibilities it holds for her career. Says Winfrey, "For me, the turn-on is the ability to express another person's life. If you can internalize, and then manifest externally the essence of another being, that is the ultimate in understanding. . . . It's almost like getting to live somebody else's life for a while, without having to experience all of the 'experience' that comes with creating another life."[18]

A Giving Spirit

With a sea of awards and accolades, it might be tough for Oprah Winfrey to discern which stand out the most. Yet it is hard to deny the magnitude of the honor Winfrey received from *Forbes* magazine in 2003. With a net worth of $1.2 billion, Winfrey was declared the first African-American woman to become a billionaire, putting her in the company of such moguls as Bill Gates and Warren Buffett. (Today Winfrey's net worth is closer to $2.7 billion.[1]) Yet though Winfrey has amassed a major fortune, she finds the greatest joy in giving it to worthy causes and people she cares about. "With all this fame and money, I have to do something more than just buy shoes," Winfrey has said with her trademark humor.[2]

Winfrey may have been understating her generosity. In 2007, *BusinessWeek* named the talk show host one of the top fifty most generous philanthropists in America. According to the magazine, Winfrey has given more than $303 million throughout her lifetime to various charities—amounting to about 12 percent of her current net worth.[3] Another distinction for Winfrey's giving is the fact that she has personally donated more money to charity than any other American celebrity.

One of Winfrey's major vehicles for helping others financially has been the Oprah Winfrey Foundation. Winfrey started the private foundation in 1987 to provide monetary grants for nonprofit organizations that "offer educational opportunities and enhance the quality of life for children and families throughout the world."[4] A 2007 Fox News report stated that Winfrey's foundation boasted assets of $172 million, which are controlled and allocated solely by Winfrey—the only member of the foundation.[5]

Perhaps the most high-profile foundation initiative was the Christmas Kindness 2002 project in South Africa. For a special documentary-style episode of her talk show, Winfrey traveled to South Africa with her partner Stedman Graham, best friend Gayle King, and several members of her staff. Over a period of twenty-one days, the group visited numerous orphanages and schools to distribute Christmas gifts, food, clothes, shoes, school supplies, and books. Along with benefiting more than fifty thousand children, Winfrey was also able to bring worldwide attention to the AIDS epidemic and poverty affecting these areas. After the show aired, the public contributed an additional $15 million to the cause.

"As the kids entered, I could see their eyes light up and their sorrows fall away while they took in the wonder— jesters, fairies in lavender tulle, and silver bubbles floating everywhere," Winfrey wrote on her Web site. "You could touch the joy they felt that someone had thought of them.

A little boy accepts a Christmas gift from Winfrey as she visits his orphanage in South Africa in 2002. She has donated millions of dollars to various charities in the country.

In that moment in Johannesburg, I thanked God that I was born to see that kind of happiness."[6]

As with many of her charitable deeds, Winfrey had been inspired to spread "Christmas Kindness" based on her own past experiences. When Winfrey was twelve years old, her mother was unable to afford Christmas gifts that year. Winfrey felt discouraged and worried about what to tell her friends when asked about what was under the tree for Christmas. Yet her hope was renewed when several nuns unexpectedly donated some toys, a fruit basket, a turkey, and a special doll for Winfrey. "I felt such a sense of relief that I would no longer have to be embarrassed when I returned to school," Winfrey remembered. "I remember feeling that I mattered enough to these nuns—whom I had never met and to this day still don't know their names— and what it meant that they had remembered me."[7]

Winfrey's childhood also inspired another major undertaking for the Oprah Winfrey Foundation: the Oprah Winfrey Boys and Girls Club of Kosciusko/ Attala County. In an effort to give back to her Mississippi hometown, Winfrey sought to build a brand-new facility for the organization, which provides well-rounded after-school programs for kids. Revealed in September 2006, the new center stood at more than 30,000 square feet and cost $5 million. Among the features were a music room, arts center, library, computer labs—as well as a kitchen in which Winfrey's personal chef gave the kids a private cooking lesson.[8] "This center belongs to you," Winfrey told those who attended the dedication ceremony. "And I want you to nurture it, support it, take care of it, and lift it up."[9]

Another nonprofit after-school program that has been touched by Winfrey's kindness is the U.S. Dream Academy. Formed to keep at-risk youth out of jail, the Dream Academy has locations in ten major cities around the country. Through mentoring, skills training, and character-building programs, the organization provides "dream building" for kids who may have parents in jail or other issues at home. In June 2008, Winfrey personally donated nine hundred thousand dollars to match total contributions given at the Dream Academy's annual "Power of a Dream Gala," which was attended by stars such as Chris Tucker, Keyshia Cole, and Peabo Bryson. Winfrey also pledged to match up to an additional five hundred thousand dollars for any donations made after the gala celebration.[10] "Oprah understands the power of dreams and how having them can positively alter a person's journey," said founder Wintley Phipps in recognition.[11]

Yet the primary focus of the Oprah Winfrey Foundation has been on education. Her many school gifts have ranged from the exclusive Miss Porter's School in Connecticut to the innovative Ron Clark Academy in Atlanta's inner city. One recurring recipient of her generosity has been Morehouse College, an all-male school that was ranked number one in educating African-American students by *Black Enterprise* magazine.[12] (Among its noted alumni are Spike Lee and Martin Luther King, Jr.) Over the years, Winfrey has given more than $12 million to the school through the Oprah Winfrey Endowed Scholarship Fund. "My dream was—when I first started making money—to pass it on and I wanted to put 100 men through Morehouse," Winfrey has said. "Right now, we're at 250 [scholarships given] and I want to make it one thousand."[13]

As Winfrey's personal charity, the Oprah Winfrey Foundation has provided hundreds of grants to worthy recipients around the globe. Yet Winfrey does not rest on the power of her own generosity; she is also dedicated to inspiring others to give their time, energy, and funds to deserving causes. To that end, Winfrey created Oprah's Angel Network. In what later became a public charity, the project began on a 1997 episode of *The Oprah Winfrey Show* in which Winfrey asked viewers to use their lives to make a difference for others. The show featured the "World's Largest Piggy Bank," which had viewers donate spare change to send fifty students to college,[14] and "Build an Oprah House," which had groups of viewers in two hundred cities build houses for Habitat for Humanity.

Through the Angel Network, Winfrey has succeeded in getting people involved in community and global giving to the tune of more than $80 million. For her part, Winfrey covers all operating costs so that 100 percent of all donations can go directly to the designated recipients. "I have a blessed life, and I have always shared my life's gifts with others," Winfrey told *BusinessWeek* in 2004. "I believe that to whom much is given, much is expected. So, I will continue to use my voice and my life as a catalyst for change, inspiring and encouraging people to help make a difference in the lives of others."[15]

In 2000, Oprah's Angel Network introduced the popular "Use Your Life" award program. Thanks to viewer donations, more than fifty community do-gooders received grants of a hundred thousand dollars for their respective organizations.[16] The program ran for three years and benefited a diverse group of organizations, including One Heartland, a summer camp for kids with the HIV virus; Bicycles and Ideas for Kids' Empowerment (B.I.K.E.), a cycling program for inner-city children; and the Garden Project, which provides rewarding work for prisoners on farmland. (The founders of both the aforementioned U.S. Dream Academy and Ron Clark Academy also started out as "Use Your Life" award winners, later inspiring Winfrey to give further funds through her personal foundation.)

Oprah's "angels" were also on call in 2005, when Hurricanes Katrina and Rita wreaked serious havoc on the United State's Gulf Coast. Many families lost everything in this catastrophic natural disaster, and much help was needed in the region. At Winfrey's urging, viewers donated more than $15.6 million to the rebuilding of homes and

The city of New Orleans in Louisiana was completely flooded by 2005's Hurricane Katrina. It was one of the worst hit areas. Winfrey helped raise millions of dollars for the relief effort.

communities in Mississippi, Louisiana, Alabama, and Texas. (Rock star Jon Bon Jovi even donated 1 million dollars of his own money to help out!) Thanks to the Angel Network, more than a thousand families were able to return home and enjoy new living spaces, parks, and playgrounds. Also, in partnership with First Book, more than 5 million books were distributed to schools and libraries throughout the Gulf Coast.[17]

Winfrey's love of books has also shone through in another Angel Network initiative: the Oprah's Book Club Awards. In a creative manner of giving, the awards provide books to needy children who live in the actual physical settings of various book club selections. In the past, children in Beijing, China, were given books in honor of Pearl S. Buck's *The Good Earth* and in St. Petersburg, Russia, in honor of Leo Tolstoy's *Anna Karenina.*[18]

Along with education and enrichment, Oprah's Angel Network has also put a heavy focus on leadership and empowerment. In 2007, the Angel Network launched the O Ambassadors program in tandem with Free the Children (a past grant recipient in 2002). That year, more than ten thousand youth became O Ambassadors and pledged to take action toward addressing the world's most pressing issues: poverty, education, health, and the environment. Working toward goals set by the United Nations for the year 2015, the ambassadors participate in clubs and school-based activities designed to promote stronger citizenship and leadership. "It is hard to believe that there are millions of people who still don't have access to food, clean water, or medical care," Winfrey wrote on the O Ambassadors Web site. "But I am encouraged by the spirit of the young people in the United States and Canada who feel the obligation to help their global neighbors. To give of themselves. And to inspire others to do the same."[19]

Indeed, Winfrey has inspired many to follow in her own giving footsteps. Along with the projects mentioned in this chapter, her foundation and Angel Network have also helped build women's shelters, community and youth centers, schools, and much more. It is clear that the impact and reach of Winfrey's philanthropic efforts have been substantial; yet for Winfrey, giving is just part of everyday existence. Says Winfrey, "So many things in life inspire philanthropy, such as your faith in humanity and your belief in the human spirit to overcome."[20]

6

The Revolution Will Be Televised

Viewers who watched *The Oprah Winfrey Show* on September 13, 2004, may have thought they had accidentally tuned into a game show, such as *The Price Is Right*. After all, it is not every day that Winfrey gives away cars to every single member of her studio audience! For the premiere episode of the show's nineteenth season, Winfrey arranged to have 276 brand-new, fully-loaded Pontiac G6 sedans—each worth $28,400—as a surprise gift for the viewers in attendance.

In true Oprah Winfrey style, the buildup was big. (The show even had two emergency medical technicians on hand just in case someone fainted![1]) Titled "Wildest

Dreams With Oprah Winfrey," the show started with Winfrey surprising eleven people who had written in to the show about their car woes with free Pontiacs. At the end of the segment, Winfrey announced that one more surprise recipient would be picked from the audience. Later the audience was given tiny gift boxes and told by Winfrey that one box held a key for the lucky winner. Yet as the audience tore open the boxes, they got the surprise of their lives: "*You* get a car! *You* get a car! *You* get a car! *Everybody gets a car!* Is that the wildest? Isn't it stunning? And guess what? Your cars are waiting outside!" exclaimed Winfrey, after which the screaming audience flocked outside to see a parking lot full of cars topped with red bows.

Winfrey and her staff had put months of preparation into this giant surprise, with Winfrey even making a special trip to the GM plant in Michigan for a test drive.[2] Unbeknownst to the audience, each person had been specially selected after family and friends told show producers they needed new cars. (One teen said his mom's car looked "like she got in a gunfight," while another couple had a combined four hundred thousand miles on their two cars.[3]) The cars were not the only surprise on that show: Winfrey gave a $130,000 check to a large family on the verge of eviction, and she also gave a Pontiac G6, full college scholarship, makeover from Tyra Banks, and ten thousand dollars in new clothes to a twenty-year-old former foster kid. "We're calling this our wildest dream season, because this year on the *Oprah* show, no dream is too wild, no surprise too impossible to pull off," Winfrey told viewers.[4]

Though it is hard to imagine matching the excitement generated by Winfrey's car giveaway, Winfrey has managed to do it regularly with her famed "Oprah's Favorite Things" episode. Airing during the holiday season, the special show features Winfrey showing off must-have gifts of the year and bestowing them upon the live studio audience. Since the festivities first kicked off in 2002, Winfrey has featured products ranging from BlackBerrys to Ugg boots to Burberry cashmere scarves. Much like the "cars" episode, audiences are typically preselected in secret to reward special groups, such as teachers and volunteers.

In 2006, Winfrey decided to switch up the "Favorite Things" format. In what Winfrey dubbed her "Favorite Giveaway Ever," Winfrey chose not to pass out the typical luxury gifts and instead gave the audience free camcorders and debit cards worth a thousand dollars. Rather than using the money for their own benefit, the audience was challenged to donate or to do a good deed with the money—and use the camcorder to document the experience. The results of the "Pay It Forward Challenge" were featured on a later show with impressive outcomes. Many audience members had reached out to their communities to multiply the money and to do even more good. Among them were sisters Kasey Osborne and Kristy O'Connor, who drummed up two hundred thousand dollars for a Chicago women's shelter in just one week; Minnie Scheidt, who raised seventy thousand dollars for the family of a father afflicted with a deadly brain tumor; and Megan O'Gorman, whose donation to a Hawaii children's hospital of four airplane tickets turned into forty airfares donated by Go! Airlines.[5]

Though Winfrey returned to the standard "Favorite Things" format in 2007, she again deviated from the norm in 2008. In light of the shaky U.S. economy, Winfrey introduced "Oprah's Favorite Things . . . With a Twist!" Rather than giving away gifts, Winfrey showed off inexpensive items that were less about spending and more about sentiment. Among the ideas were homegrown fruit and veggie baskets, "re-gifting" parties, and "gratitude boxes" filled with personal notes. "A few years ago at my Happy 50th Birthday luncheon, my friends wrote me heartfelt notes that they then placed inside this silver box," Winfrey shared on the air. "The words from your heart mean more to people than anything you can buy."[6]

Though Winfrey is known for treating live studio audiences to her generosity, Winfrey's kindness also continues behind the scenes. Her staff is quite often on the receiving end of Winfrey's giving nature, one notable example being a Hawaiian vacation in celebration of the show's twentieth anniversary in 2006. For the occasion, Winfrey chartered five jets to take her staff and their families to Maui, with 1,065 people total going on the trip. In 2009, Winfrey topped herself by taking her entire staff and their families on a two-week Mediterranean cruise adventure.

Christmas is also a major time of giving for the *Oprah* team, with producers receiving gifts such as diamond earrings and luggage with ten-thousand-dollar gift certificates hidden inside. One legendary story tells of Winfrey giving her assistant a Jeep brochure, promptly followed by honking outside the window. The assistant looked outside to see a brand-new Jeep Grand Cherokee with Winfrey's theme song coming from its speakers.[7]

Another tale of Winfrey's generosity to staff centers on the 1988 wedding of show producer Mary Kay Clinton. Not only was Winfrey the designated maid of honor, but she also paid for the entire wedding and reception. Guests enjoyed steak and lobster at the wedding dinner, while trumpets announced the arrival of the bride on a horse-drawn carriage.[8] Clinton was extremely grateful for the financial and emotional support of her close friend Oprah Winfrey, for whom Clinton has told interviewers she would "take a bullet."[9]

Much as Winfrey likes to celebrate her loyal viewers and staff, those whose lives she has touched also return their appreciation in innovative ways. For Winfrey's fiftieth birthday in 2004, the producers banned Winfrey from the studio while they made top-secret preparations for the big celebratory show. ("I'm feeling a little out of sorts here because I have no control," Winfrey confessed later to the audience.[10]) On the show, Winfrey received serenades of "Happy Birthday" from Stevie Wonder and "Simply the Best" from Tina Turner, as well as a four-hundred-pound banana cake from Jay Leno. Video messages were also shown from celebrities like Jennifer Lopez, Celine Dion, and Will Smith, as well as Nelson Mandela and South African children.[11] Also among the taped tributes were Reverend Jesse Jackson ("She's as original to America as jazz"), John Travolta ("Oprah has taught the world how to listen and to face some of the most important issues of our time"), and Vivica A. Fox ("Oprah's imprint on the world for her first 50 years has been nothing short of amazing").[12]

The celebrations thrown by her friends, family, and loved ones continued well past the show, with festivities in Chicago, Los Angeles, and Montecito, California. In Chicago, Stedman Graham threw a private party for Winfrey and seventy-five guests at the top of the Sears Tower. Some of the guests in attendance included Martin Luther King Jr.'s widow Coretta Scott King, Winfrey's best friend Gayle King, and jazz musician Ramsey Lewis, who played "Happy Birthday" for Winfrey.[13] Winfrey's father also gave a speech in which he fondly shared stories about Oprah's first public speaking experiences in church.[14]

Winfrey then jetted out to California for the weekend, where she lunched with fifty of her closest lady friends at the Hotel Bel-Air on Friday. (Among the attendees were Ellen DeGeneres, Salma Hayek, and Toni Morrison.) At the luncheon, Winfrey was presented with a reading of the poem "Continue," which her close friend and mentor Maya Angelou had written especially for the occasion. On Saturday, Winfrey continued the celebration with a major bash—the centerpiece of which was a chocolate raspberry cake covered in 23-karat gold. Surrounded by such celebrity friends as Tom Hanks, John Travolta, and Stevie Wonder, Winfrey hopped on the microphone and said in wonderment: "Have you ever, ever seen anything like this?"[15]

All the well-wishes, parties, and tributes left no doubt that Winfrey was a loved and revered figure among many, a fact that did not go unnoticed by her partner Stedman Graham: "I think she's amazing," Graham told *EXTRA*. "I think she's just beginning; she has a vision larger than the show. She wants to make an impact around the world."[16]

While Winfrey's talk show has often acted as a means to that end, Winfrey took it one step further in 2008 by introducing a reality show titled *Oprah's Big Give*. The first prime-time series produced by Harpo, the show featured ten contestants traveling the country with the motto "Give Big or Go Home." (Contestants ranged from a wheelchair-bound media executive to a dot-com

A scene from the first and only season of *Oprah's Big Give* shows contestants receiving large sums of money to be put to use for the benefit of others.

millionaire to a beauty pageant queen.) Throughout the competition, the contestants were given money and resources and challenged to find powerful ways to use them for the good of others. The winner, Stephen Paletta, was given 1 million dollars—half of which to keep and the other half to give to worthy causes.

With the prize money, Paletta created a nonprofit organization called Stephen's Journey Foundation. Using various forms of media, his foundation helps shed light on socially conscious organizations around the world with the aim of raising money and awareness for their causes.

And in the same vein, Winfrey urged viewers of *Oprah's Big Give* to go forth as Paletta had and give big. "It is my deepest hope that all of you who have watched this over the weeks will continue giving and that giving and giving and giving becomes a national movement," Winfrey stated on the show's finale.[17]

Indeed, Winfrey has successfully used her status as a television personality to inspire generosity in others as well as provided a much-needed forum for good deeds and pressing needs. In this realm, Winfrey finds her job rewarding for reasons far beyond the millions she gets paid—in fact, Winfrey happily puts in fourteen-hour days on a regular basis. "It's not work," Winfrey has said. "Steve Martin has a joke about how some people go to the drugstore, and they sell Flair pens. And he says, in a silly voice, 'And I get *paid* for doing this!' I feel the same way. I feel like I would do this if I didn't get a dime for it, and that's why you know you are doing the right thing—because it doesn't even feel like work."[18]

7

Champion of Others

Along with donating considerable funds to causes close to her heart, Oprah Winfrey also offers her valuable time and energy. A tireless advocate for those less fortunate, Winfrey pulls from her own experiences and deep well of compassion to make a difference on such issues as gun control, lack of education, the AIDS epidemic, and racism. Another issue of great importance to Winfrey is child abuse: "If I could change just one thing, I would stop people from beating their kids. Not just beating, but molesting kids, verbally abusing kids, neglecting kids," Winfrey has said. "The dishonor of children is the single worst problem in this country. If we ended it, there would be an incredible ripple effect on society."[1]

On a 1990 episode of her talk show, Winfrey publicly declared her own experiences with abuse. The show featured a woman named Truddi Chase, who had developed multiple personality disorder as a result of being physically and sexually abused from a young age. Though Winfrey was set to discuss Chase's book *When Rabbit Howls,* Winfrey instead broke into tears and shared her own story of molestation with the audience. "It happened on the air in the middle of someone else's experience, and I thought I was going to have a breakdown on television," Winfrey told *USA Today.* "And I said, 'Stop! Stop! You've got to stop rolling cameras!' And they didn't, so I got myself through it, but it was really quite [upsetting] for me."[2]

After that cathartic experience, Winfrey set an intention to take an active stance against abuse. That year, she introduced "Year of the Child" segments on her show designed to raise awareness of the various plights of children around the world. In 1991, she testified before the U.S. Senate Judiciary Committee in favor of the National Child Protection Act. The goal of the act was to establish a national database of convicted child abusers. President Bill Clinton signed the act into a law in 1993, after which it became widely known as the "Oprah Bill."

Winfrey looks on as President Bill Clinton signs the National Child Protection Act on December 20, 1993.

In 1992, Winfrey broke the silence yet again with a television documentary titled *Scared Silent*. Winfrey introduced the film by telling her own story and urging those being abused to get help. (The importance of the message was underscored by the fact that all three broadcast networks carried the film at the same time—a first.[3]) Winfrey also went on a media tour to promote the cause, appearing on *Good Morning America, This Morning,* and *The Today Show.*[4] The response was massive: 45 million people watched the film, and tens of thousands of calls flooded into the special hotlines set up for victims.

Winfrey felt heartened to see so many reaching out for hope and expressed her belief that the film "empowered children and adult children everywhere, so they know they do not have to stand alone. It's time to stop the pain and suffering of children, and make the world a safer place for all of us."[5]

In 2005, Winfrey took her efforts one step further by setting up a "Child Predator Watch List" Web site and campaign. She personally offered a hundred-thousand-dollar reward to any viewer who could provide the FBI with information leading to the capture of sex offenders featured on Winfrey's Web site and show. "The children of this nation are being stolen, raped, tortured and killed by sexual predators who are walking right into your homes," said Winfrey on the show. "I have had *enough*. With every breath in my body, whatever it takes and, most importantly, with you by my side, we are going to move heaven and earth to stop an evil that's been going on for far too long."[6] The campaign was effective—within forty-eight hours of the launch, two of the featured predators were captured. Since then, seven additional sex offenders from Winfrey's watch list have also been brought to justice.[7]

In September 2008, Winfrey continued her crusade with a special episode dedicated to the Protect Our Children Act under consideration by the U.S. Senate. Winfrey used the show to urge viewers to express their support of the bill to their senators. Throughout the show,

Winfrey also educated viewers on disturbing new trends in child pornography and ways for parents to protect their children.[8]

Winfrey's painful past has translated into not only a deep passion for prevention, but also a means of forging powerful bonds with others. One of the most significant connections Winfrey has made in this realm is with writer and poet Maya Angelou. Winfrey had felt profoundly drawn to Angelou ever since first reading *I Know Why the Caged Bird Sings* as a teenager, remembering the experience as "my first recollection of being validated. The fact that someone as poor as I, as black as I, from the South, from rape, from confusion, could move to hope, to possibility, and to victory, could be written about in a real book that I had chosen in the library was amazing to me," Winfrey has said.[9]

Along with having endured eerily similar backgrounds, the two women also possess a great degree of inner strength and shared appreciation for black history. Over the years, Winfrey and Angelou became not only colleagues and close friends, but also like family—in fact, Winfrey has stated that she believes Angelou "was my mother in another life. I love her deeply."[10]

In 1997, Winfrey chose Angelou's *The Heart of a Woman* as one of her Oprah's Book Club selections. Instead of taping a discussion inside the studio, Angelou hosted Winfrey and several viewers at her North Carolina home for a home-cooked meal and pajama party.[11] Along with honoring her books, Winfrey has also found other creative ways to show her admiration for Angelou. She has thrown Angelou a number of lavish birthday parties, including a North Carolina soiree in which Winfrey flew in partygoers from all over the world and a Mexican cruise for Angelou and seventy of her friends. And the admiration is mutual: "Oprah, beautiful, tough and bodacious, is the kind of daughter I would have wanted to have," Angelou has stated.[12]

In 1993, Winfrey and Angelou starred together in the ABC television movie *There Are No Children Here.* Respectively, the pair played a single mother and grandmother living in the Chicago projects. Based on a real-life story and setting, the film addressed heart-wrenching issues of poverty and violence plaguing families in the inner city. Behind the scenes, Winfrey went above and beyond for many members of the cast, promising a Disneyland trip to young actors who earned straight "A" grades on their report card. She also sent one twelve-year-old cast member to private school and helped the rest of her family secure jobs. Winfrey's entire salary of five hundred thousand dollars was donated to a scholarship fund, with the money being matched by ABC.[13]

For Winfrey, it was extremely gratifying to help those whose lives resembled the story off camera: "You find people in the projects who have as much desire for fulfillment and enrichment—to be somebody—as anywhere in the world," Winfrey told *Jet* magazine.[14]

Though significant, the film was far from the first time Winfrey had taken an active stance against pervasive issues that affect African Americans. One of her earliest talk show episodes bravely explored the idea that racism is still alive and well by filming in all-white Forsyth County, Georgia. During the taping, many of the town's residents used offensive racial slurs in describing to Winfrey why no African Americans had been allowed in the area since 1912. As a result of that experience, Winfrey realized she did not want to provide a forum for such toxic beliefs: "I felt in the early years of my career that it was necessary for me as an African American to challenge anybody who was saying anything about black people," Winfrey told *Good Morning America* in 2005. "And then . . . I realized I was not doing myself nor anyone else any good."[15]

Winfrey's willingness to take on what some consider unfashionable or controversial topics was a big part of what made her stand out early in her career. Along with tackling racism, Winfrey also addressed issues of homophobia and the AIDS epidemic in the 1980s—when such topics were still somewhat taboo. In 1986, Winfrey interviewed legendary pianist Liberace two months before he died of AIDS. A later episode featured audience members coming out of the closet by standing up one by one and announcing that they were gay. On yet another episode, Winfrey shone the spotlight on a West Virginia town known for shunning gays and those with AIDS. Winfrey minced no words in her opinion of the town's closed-minded views: "I hear this is a God-fearing town. Where's all that Christian love and understanding?"[16]

Part of Winfrey's conviction may have stemmed from her own personal experiences off camera. In 1988, Winfrey's friend and longtime staff member Billy Rizzo passed away of AIDS; just a year later, Winfrey's half brother Jeffrey Lee also died of the disease. In recent years, Winfrey has also taken much-needed steps to help alleviate the AIDS crisis in South Africa. (Experts estimate that 5.4 million South Africans are infected with the HIV virus.) To encourage AIDS testing, Winfrey publicly took an AIDS test in early 2007 and promised free AIDS testing, counseling, and treatment to students at her South African leadership academy. "To be a great leader, you must be of sound mind, body, and spirit," Winfrey told the girls. "Part of leadership is having the courage to demonstrate true action. Today I have taken the test to demonstrate why it's so important."[17]

Winfrey's heartfelt actions and extraordinary citizenship have not gone unnoticed.

In 2002, Winfrey was the first person ever to receive the Bob Hope Humanitarian Award given at the Fifty-fifth Annual Primetime Emmy Awards. (Later recipients included Bill Cosby and St. Jude's Children's Hospital

Winfrey and Elie Wiesel socialize at the Elie Wiesel Foundation for Humanity Gala in New York, May 20, 2007, where Winfrey was honored with the foundation's Humanitarian Award.

founder Danny Thomas.) After receiving the award from Tom Hanks, Winfrey addressed everyone who had helped her reach her peak: "I feel like I should be giving this award to the people who have supported me for over 18 years on this most amazing journey. . . . There really is nothing more important to me than striving to be a good human being, so to be here tonight and be acknowledged as the first to receive this honor is beyond expression in words for me."[18]

Winfrey was again singled out for her humanitarian efforts in 2007 when she received the Elie Wiesel Foundation's Humanitarian Award. In the past, Winfrey had featured Wiesel's book *Night* in her book club as well as accompanied the Holocaust survivor to the former concentration camp Auschwitz on her talk show. In honoring Winfrey, Wiesel's admiration was clear: "Vision, authenticity, and greatness—you say 'Oprah' and these words spring to your mind. Oprah the public figure and Oprah the friend are one and the same person, never violating the covenant she made with society: to help the helpless and give a voice to the voiceless."[19]

8

The Church of O

It was just after the World Trade Center terrorist attacks of September 11, 2001, and Oprah Winfrey had responded with America Under Attack themed show topics such as "Is War the Only Answer?" and "How To Talk to Kids."[1] Yet perhaps the most impactful message Winfrey sent during the disaster's aftermath came not on the air but from the pulpit. On September 23, 2001, Winfrey hosted an interfaith ceremony at New York's Yankee Stadium for twenty thousand people. Mayor Rudy Giuliani also spoke, alongside moving performances by Bette Midler and Placido Domingo. "I believe when you lose a loved one, you gain an angel whose name you know," Winfrey told the crowd.[2] "Let not one single life have passed in vain. What really matters is who you love and how you love."[3]

For Winfrey, who had spent much of her childhood speaking at church, it was second nature to hold a service dedicated to unity and faith in the face of despair. It was also a familiar role for her fans and followers, who had come to see Winfrey as somewhat of a spiritual guru in recent years. A 2002 *Christianity Today* article titled "The Church of O" may have put the shift of perception best: "Since 1994, when she abandoned traditional talk-show fare for more edifying content, and 1998, when she began 'Change Your Life TV,' Oprah's most significant role has become that of spiritual leader," wrote LaTonya Taylor. "To her audience of more than 22 million mostly female viewers, she has become a postmodern priestess—an icon of church-free spirituality."[4]

Many of Winfrey's own adult beliefs began to form after she read minister Eric Butterworth's book, *Discover the Power Within You.* Butterworth's theory that God resides in every individual resonated with Winfrey, who later told audiences, "This book changed my perspective on life and religion. Eric Butterworth teaches that God isn't 'up there.' He exists inside each one of us, and it's up to us to seek the divine within."[5] Though Winfrey did not embrace Butterworth's message until her later years, her way of worship had reflected this style of thought since she was a young child—offering herself as a vessel with the

New York Governor George Pataki hugs Winfrey after she gave a speech at Yankee Stadium September 23, 2001, commemorating the victims of the September 11 terrorist attacks. On Winfrey's right, New York City Mayor Rudolph Giuliani and Senator Charles Schumer applaud.

following prayer: "*Use me, God. Show me how to take who I am, who I want to be, and what I can do, and use it for a purpose greater than myself.*"

To that end, Winfrey has used her talk show as a platform to positively reach and to inspire millions of people. In the mid-1990s, Winfrey's "Remember Your Spirit" and "Change Your Life TV" themes marked a notable departure from many of the other talk shows on the air. While shows hosted by Jerry Springer, Ricki Lake, and Maury Povich often focused on conflict-oriented stories, Winfrey turned the audience's focus inward with messages of empowerment, healing, and change. "It's time to move on from 'We are dysfunctional' to 'What are we going to do about it?'" Winfrey has said.[6]

To help her viewers take that step, Winfrey began to regularly feature self-help and spirituality gurus on the show. One such expert was Gary Zukav, whose book *The Seat of the Soul* examines the human soul from a scientific standpoint. According to *Publishers Weekly*, Winfrey received so much mail about Zukav that she featured him for a full hour again in April 1999—along with several viewers who testified how the book had changed their lives. Zukav became a fixture on the show, and the "Oprah factor" was clear: the book skyrocketed to 1.7 million copies in print.[7]

Another expert who shot to stardom as a by-product of Winfrey's interest was Iyanla Vanzant.

A spiritual counselor, author, and Yoruba priestess, Vanzant inspired Winfrey and her audience to the point that she was invited back monthly for "Iyanla Tuesdays." Urging viewers to reclaim their power and strength, Vanzant often weighed in on relationship topics like "Women Looking for Love." Barbara Walters took note of Vanzant, and invited her to appear on her own talk show, *The View*. In 2001, Walters went on to develop and executive produce an Oprah-esque talk show for Vanzant. Though the show was short-lived, Vanzant went on to find small-screen success as a life coach on the reality show *Starting Over*.

Along with getting viewers in touch with their spirituality, Winfrey also explored the idea of connecting viewers to actual *spirits*. In February 1998, Winfrey featured medium James Van Praagh on the show. Specializing in communication with the dead, Van Praagh spoke of his experiences conveying messages from deceased loved ones to the living. "My life's mission, I believe, is to open up people's hearts and minds and open up their awareness . . . that there is no such thing as death," Van Praagh has stated on Winfrey's radio network. "Death is definitely an illusion."[8] On the show, Winfrey presented a balanced picture of the topic—expressing her own doubts as well as inviting expert and dissenter Michael Shermer to weigh in.[9]

On April 17, 2000, Oprah Winfrey holds a press conference in New York to reveal the cover of the first issue of *O* magazine. The magazine debuted nationwide two days later and sold out quickly.

Many Oprah Winfrey-endorsed experts have also gone on to become radio talk show hosts on the Oprah Radio network. Launched in September 2006, the channel is hosted on XM Satellite Radio and features a variety of shows on topics like spirituality, health, parenting, finance, current events, and relationships. Among the hosts are Maya Angelou, design expert Nate Berkus, personal organizer Peter Walsh, Rabbi Shmuley Boteach, and spirituality author Marianne Williamson. Winfrey has also taken on hosting duties with "Oprah's Soul Series," in which Winfrey explores metaphysical ideas such as auras and soul mates.[10]

Another popular show on Oprah Radio is "Laws of Attraction Radio," which is based on a principle that has long fascinated Winfrey. In 2007, Winfrey sparked a nationwide frenzy when she introduced a book and film titled *The Secret,* which explores ways people can use the Law of Attraction to manifest their desires in life. With the theory that "thoughts become things," the creators appeared on Winfrey's show to discuss how positive thinking creates positive energy and outcomes—and the converse effects of negative thoughts. According to the creators, the "secret" could be boiled down to three simple steps: "Ask. Believe. Receive."[11]

For Winfrey, this train of thought was something she had long subscribed to in her life. "The message of the *Secret* is the message I've been trying to share with the world on my show for the past 21 years: that you are responsible for your life," Winfrey told Larry King. "I've known this since *The Color Purple*."[12] Winfrey went on to tell King how she believes her "obsession" with Alice Walker's book manifested itself into her Academy Award-nominated turn in the film *The Color Purple*. Not surprisingly, Winfrey's professed belief in *The Secret* resulted in 2 million additional book copies being printed.[13]

In January 2008, Winfrey started another phenomenon with her book club selection of Eckhart Tolle's *A New Earth*. Tolle had first caught Winfrey's attention in 1999 with his best-selling book *The Power of Now,* and Winfrey felt equally captivated by *A New Earth's* message of being alive and aware in the present moment. "I've read hundreds of books that have helped me become more spiritually attuned," Winfrey wrote on her Web site. "*A New Earth* resonated so deeply with me and caused such a shift in the way I perceived myself and all things, I couldn't not share it."[14]

Two months later, Winfrey and Tolle made headlines by teaching a ten-week "webinar" to help viewers integrate the book into their lives. Bearing the tagline "Are You Ready to Be Awakened?" the live Web series attracted 750,000 participants in its first two weeks of registration and was eventually downloaded more than 35 million times. Topics discussed included fulfilling your life's purpose, overcoming the ego, and being "one with life."

Mind, Body, and Spirit

Winfrey believes that, in order to experience spiritual well-being, one must strive for total wellness. "The ultimate in being healthy is to operate at full throttle–physically, emotionally and spiritually," she has said. To that end, Winfrey has partnered successfully with both her personal trainer Bob Greene and chef Rosie Daley to bring their message to the masses. A respected diet and fitness expert, Greene is a regular contributor to Winfrey's talk show, radio channel, and magazine; the two have also coauthored two books: *Make the Connection: Ten Steps to a Better Body and a Better Life* and its companion, *A Journal of Daily Renewal.*

Another successful collaboration for Winfrey was the 1994 cookbook she inspired, *In the Kitchen with Rosie: Oprah's Favorite Recipes.* Winfrey first met Daley at a San Diego spa and convinced her to come on board as her personal chef. After five years of working for Winfrey, Daley developed the book of low-fat delights with great success.

However, not all of Winfrey's efforts at promoting wellness have been so well received. Many of her guests have presented controversial opinions on topics ranging from child vaccination to hormone therapy, some of which conflict with the views of doctors and traditional medicine. When a 2009 *Newsweek* article posed the idea that "a lot of the advice her guests dispose on the show is just bad," Winfrey responded with the following statement: "The guests we feature often share their first-person stories in an effort to inform the audience and put a human face on topics relevant to them. . . . I believe my viewers understand the medical information presented on the show is just that–information–not an endorsement or prescription. Rather, my intention is for our viewers to take the information and engage in a dialogue with their medical practitioners about what may be right for them."[15]

Said Winfrey in retrospect, "It's been the most rewarding experience of my career to teach this book online with Eckhart Tolle and witness millions of people all over the globe awaken to their lives in such profound ways."[16]

Along with using the Internet and radio to expand her reach, Winfrey has also experienced success with the print medium. In 2000, *O* magazine hit newsstands in what a writer for *Fortune* called "the most successful magazine launch ever."[17] (Its first issue quickly sold out all 1 million copies printed, forcing the publisher to green-light five hundred thousand more copies.[18]) With an overriding theme of "Live Your Best Life," each monthly issue features none other than Winfrey on its cover. Though many of the features are typical women's magazine fare, *O* stands out by including the Winfrey-penned columns "Here We Go!" that kicks off the issue's theme, and "What I Know for Sure," in which Winfrey shares hard-earned insights.

Winfrey has also taken her magazine's message on the road numerous times with the Live Your Best Life Tour. Traveling to cities such as Tampa, Seattle, and Philadelphia, Winfrey has led a series of one-day workshops that sold out in record time—commanding $185 per ticket.[19] In each city, Winfrey got the rock-star greeting from screaming fans as she arrived by limousine.[20] "The [tour] literally brings *O, The Oprah Magazine* to life," publisher Jill Seelig told the press. "It has always been the magazine's mission to help the reader grow and become her best self and that is exactly what these workshops do. It is incredibly moving to watch the audience tap into Oprah's enthusiasm and energy to accomplish their own goals."[21]

Indeed Winfrey's audiences—from television to print to online—have strongly identified with her unique blend of spirituality. Though some Christians have criticized Winfrey for promoting New Age philosophies, many feel grateful to Winfrey for invoking spiritual curiosity and awakening it in so many. It is Winfrey's hope that this will empower her audience to truly live their best lives: "I have church with myself; I have church walking down the street," Winfrey has said. "I believe in the God force that lives inside all of us, and once you tap into that, you can do anything."[22]

A Leader in Education

If there was ever any doubt that Oprah Winfrey keeps her word, look no further for proof than the Oprah Winfrey Leadership Academy for Girls. What turned into a $40-million school for girls in South Africa all began with a simple promise! In December 2000, Winfrey met with former South African president Nelson Mandela and asked him what type of gift she could give to the nation. His response? "Build me a school."[1]

Winfrey went to work doing just that, as Mandela's mandate was highly in sync with one of her own big visions. She had long dreamt of creating a way to nurture South African girls and to change the grim realities of education in the region. (As of 2005, a UNICEF study showed that only 11 percent of South African students had Internet access, and only 24 percent of girls were going on to attend college.[2] Even more recently, figures showed that two-thirds of the 1.6 million South African children who had started school twelve years ago had dropped out.[3]) Winfrey believed that building a school could enable her to help girls rise above unfortunate circumstances, as she had. "I want this school to be a reflection of me," Winfrey told CNN in 2006. "I made a promise to Madiba [Mandela's clan name] and I intend to keep it."[4]

The selected location for the school was Henley-on-Klip, a peaceful village about an hour from the South African metropolis of Johannesburg. Winfrey's budget of $40 million was put to good use—along with state-of-the-art classroom facilities and residence halls, the school's fifty-two-acre campus would also include a yoga studio, beauty salon, and six-hundred-seat theater. Though some critics questioned the lavish accommodations, Winfrey held strong in her conviction that they were necessary. "These girls deserve to be surrounded by beauty, and beauty does inspire," Winfrey told *Newsweek*. "I wanted this to be a place of honor for them because these girls have never been treated with kindness. They've never been told they are pretty or have wonderful dimples. I wanted to hear those things as a child."[5]

Along with providing a top-notch setting for living and learning, Winfrey also wanted to ensure each facet of the school reflected her personal touch. During the five years of planning and construction, Winfrey worked tirelessly to select visual details, such as the color of the bricks and the art on display.[6] She also made sure the living conditions were luxurious, from the serving china to the oversized closets to the two-hundred-thread-count bedsheets. (Winfrey even tested each bed herself for comfort![7])

And, of course, Winfrey put the same painstaking effort into the admission process. (Of 3,500 applicants, only 152 students would initially be chosen.[8]) In the final rounds, Winfrey personally interviewed all five hundred finalists to determine leadership potential, goals, and commitment to education—as well as financial need. Hopes were high for the impact that these young leaders could make on their nation and the world as a whole: "If Oprah identifies even five future leaders of South Africa and empowers them to improve their country, millions will feel the positive ripple effects," wrote Saul Garlick, founder of the Student Movement for Real Change.[9]

Though many shared Garlick's hope for South Africa's prospects, some of Winfrey's more vocal critics wondered why Winfrey was not equally dedicated to helping inner-city youth in America. Winfrey took the opportunity to respond to her naysayers in a 2007 *Newsweek* story: "I became so frustrated with visiting inner-city schools that I just stopped going. The sense that you need to learn just isn't there," she told the magazine. "[In America], if you ask the kids what they want or need, they will say an iPod or some sneakers. In South Africa, they don't ask for money or toys. They ask for uniforms so they can go to school."[10]

And on January 2, 2007, they did just that as the Oprah Winfrey Leadership Academy for Girls opened its doors. Marking the landmark occasion was a ribbon-cutting ceremony attended by such stars as Mariah Carey, Tina Turner, Mary J. Blige, Chris Rock, Spike Lee, and Sidney Poitier. Also on hand to celebrate the milestone was Nelson

On January 2, 2007, Winfrey, surrounded by eager students, cuts the ribbon and officially opens the Oprah Winfrey Leadership Academy for Girls in Henley-on-Klip, South Africa.

Mandela. Each celebrity was asked to donate a personally meaningful book for the school's ten-thousand-book library with a personal inscription as a symbol of his or her support.[11] "[This is] a testimony to Oprah's power to see all these people who showed up to support her," said filmmaker Lee.

Along with a strong educational curriculum, the school was designed to instill strong leadership qualities and the South African principles of "ubuntu/botho" into students. (*Ubuntu/botho* are Zulu words that stand for humanity, compassion, and service to others;[12] the words mean "I am because we are.") Despite her busy schedule, Winfrey had high hopes for being extremely involved at the school and furthering its aims. Along with teaching leadership classes via satellite, Winfrey also has built a house on the school's campus—where she plans to move upon retirement. As she told *Newsweek,* "I want to be near my girls and be in a position to see how they're doing; I want to have a presence they can sense and feel comfortable with."[13]

However, it was not long before Winfrey's vision was tainted by scandal. In late 2007, allegations arose that students were being physically and sexually abused by a dorm matron. Upon hearing the news, Winfrey immediately traveled to South Africa to address the situation. She personally reached out to all the affected families—who showed her the same compassion that she has shown so many. "It's not your fault. We don't blame you," one father said to Winfrey. "You trusted them. You have more passion for the school and its existence than anyone else in this country, including us parents."[14]

For Winfrey, the shocking turn of events was especially hard to handle in light of her own painful past with sexual abuse. Having sought to provide a safe haven for girls, Winfrey felt betrayed and angry—calling the scandal "one of the most devastating, if not the most devastating, experiences of my life."[15] Winfrey then went to great measures to prevent future instances of abuse, providing all students with counseling and cell phones programmed with her own contact information. "I am a mama bear when it comes to protecting my children, and these girls are like my children," Winfrey told reporters in a press conference.

Though the issue had temporarily tarnished her dream, Winfrey held strong to her ideals and original goals for the school. "What I know is that no one—not the accused nor any persons—can destroy the dream that I have held and the dream that each girl continues to hold for herself at the school," Winfrey told *Time*. "I am prepared to do whatever is necessary to make sure that the Oprah Winfrey Leadership Academy for Girls becomes the safe and nurturing and enriched setting that I have envisioned, a place capable of fostering a full measure of these girls' productivity, creativity and of their humanity."[16]

Oprah's Angel Network poured its efforts into opening another South African school in the small town of Kokstad.

Nelson Mandela

Nelson Mandela is a revered world leader who has devoted his life to the struggle against apartheid. Mandela's given name is Rolihlahla, which means "pulling the branch of the tree" or "troublemaker." Although the name "Nelson" was given to him upon entering school, Mandela has embodied the essence of his original name by bringing lasting change to his country.

After studying law, Mandela got involved in politics by joining the African National Congress in 1944. In 1948, the National Party's apartheid policies came into power and Mandela joined the resistance. Through grassroots and underground efforts, Mandela organized youth to fight for the liberation of blacks. In 1963, Mandela was arrested on such charges as sabatoge and sentenced to life in prison on Robben Island.

"During my lifetime, I have dedicated myself to the struggle of the African people," Mandela said before going to prison. "I have fought against white domination, and I have fought against black domination. I have cherished the ideal of a democratic and free society in which all persons live together in harmony and with equal opportunities. It is an ideal which I hope to live for and to achieve. But, if need be, it is an ideal for which I am prepared to die."[17]

Mandela's popularity grew in prison as he came to symbolize freedom, and after serving twenty-seven years, he was finally released by President Frederik Willem de Klerk. In 1993, Mandela was awarded the Nobel Peace Prize and elected the first black president of South Africa through a democratic election. Though Mandela retired from the presidency in 1999, retirement has not slowed his struggle to help his people. He continues to inspire others to join the fight to make the world better, including Winfrey. "His grace and wisdom make me want to be a better human being," she has said.[18]

Named the Seven Fountains Primary School, the Kokstad school became a $1.6-million project that would serve a thousand boys and girls. Winfrey first became familiar with the school in 2002, when it was located on a farm with limited electricity and running water. At the time, all the windows were broken, the floors were made of dirt, and the teachers were forced to run classes without pens or paper.[19] After that visit, Winfrey made it her mission to provide the students with better circumstances: "We thought the school you had before was not good enough, so we wanted to build the best school for you," Winfrey told students.[20]

Opened in March 2007, the new Seven Fountains featured twenty-five classrooms, three multi-purpose rooms, library, computer lab, sports fields, and a playground. The school was built to be eco-friendly and energy efficient, using solar power and a recycled water system. A garden was also built to provide vegetables that could be used in school meals.[21] In light of the school's success, a similar school, Vele High School in Limpopo, is expected to open in 2010.

The schools were made possible by donations from Oprah's Angel Network, which over the years has built sixty-plus schools in thirteen countries. Along with funding and creating schools, the Angel Network also provides books to children around the world and grants to various organizations. Grant recipients have ranged from

Free the Children, which used the grant to give children in a Chinese mountain village access to education, to the American Library Association's Great Stories Club, which provides books to at-risk teenagers.

Another way Winfrey demonstrates her commitment to education is through the Oprah Winfrey Scholars Program. Run through the Oprah Winfrey Foundation, the program provides scholarships to students who want to use their education to benefit their communities.[22] The program also partnered with the Robert F. Wagner Graduate School of Public Service to provide $2.5 million in funding that would enable disadvantaged African women to enroll. In exchange for receiving tuition, housing, meals, books, supplies, and travel, the students were required to take their learnings back to their native countries after graduation. "The fund will be established to help strong women become leaders in Africa, giving them a greater voice in their own lives," Winfrey has said.[23]

Of the many causes and organizations that Winfrey supports, education will always be among her top priorities. Providing the means for underprivileged students to receive schooling is extremely meaningful for Winfrey, who has said: "Because of what reading and learning has done for me, I believe that education is the door to freedom, that it changes everything."[24]

10

A Lasting Legacy

Media experts speak of the "Oprah-fication" of society, and her birthplace of Kosciusko, Mississippi, is no exception. The dirt road that once housed the farm where Winfrey was raised is now known as Oprah Winfrey Road and is a popular destination for visitors to the area. Though the house is no longer intact, a sign resides in its place with Winfrey's biographical information and directions to her former church.

Though Winfrey has come a long way, her roots are still an integral part of her being. Despite a far-from-idyllic childhood, Winfrey credits her upbringing with the qualities that have made her successful—among them perseverance, faith, resourcefulness, and compassion. From Winfrey's point of view, her trials have ultimately enabled her to triumph. "Somewhere I've always known that I was born for greatness in my life," Winfrey once told Barbara Walters. "I remember being on my grandmother's farm and knowing at four years old—I just always knew. I don't regret being born illegitimately and living [different] parts of my life with my grandmother, my father, [and] my mother. I don't regret all that past confusion. . . . It has made me

Oprah Winfrey's life exemplifies the American dream. Through hard work, she has risen above poverty to become one of the most successful people in the world.

Legacies and Legends

In 2005, Winfrey paid tribute in grand fashion to her own inspirations by holding the Legends Ball—a black-and-white gala devoted to honoring twenty-five inspiring African-American women. (Among the honorees were Tina Turner, Maya Angelou, Diana Ross, Coretta Scott King, Aretha Franklin, and Patti LaBelle.) Attended by four hundred guests, the all-weekend affair was simply spectacular.

The weekend kicked off with a luncheon designed to meld the old and new with a "Legends and Young'uns" theme. While lunching at Winfrey's California estate, the ladies enjoyed music by John Legend and tasty treats like minted pea soup, pistachio-covered chicken, and chocolate cake with truffle cream. Seating was alternated around the table so that the "young'uns" could gain valuable wisdom from the "legends." Afterward, young'uns like Alicia Keys, Janet Jackson, and Mariah Carey were quick to return the favor, honoring them by presenting Pearl Cleage's poem "We Speak Your Names."

Other highlights of the weekend included a lively gospel brunch and swanky "white-tie" ball held at Santa Barbara's Bacara Resort and Spa. White-attired attendees included then-Senator Barack Obama, Barbra Streisand, Sidney Poitier, Tom Cruise, and Barbara Walters. For Winfrey, who had spent a year planning the big occasion, it was "truly one of the greatest moments of her life"[1] to honor her accomplished peers. "These women, who have been meaningful to so many of us over the years, are legends who have been magnificent in their pioneering and advancing of African-American women," Winfrey said. "It is because of their steps that our journey has no boundaries."[2]

exactly who I am, and without all those elements, I would be somebody else."[3]

Another major "element" Winfrey carries with her from childhood is her close connection to the spiritual realm. Although some fans have elevated Winfrey to an almost God-like status, she continues to stay grounded and to maintain her own faith. "One Sunday, I was in church, and a deacon tapped me on the knee and asked for my autograph," Winfrey once told *Christianity Today*. "I told him, 'I don't do autographs in church. Jesus is the star here.'"[4]

While Winfrey remains humble about her celebrity, she is undeniably a superstar to the rest of the world. Winfrey's Web site averages 92 million pages views every month,[5] and *O* magazine is the third-most popular on the newsstand.[6] Her show also continues to be number one—as broadcast in 140 countries globally and seen by 44 million viewers each week in just the United States.[7]

Having earned dozens of awards, from Daytime Emmys to People's Choice Awards, Winfrey's most high-profile honor may have been 1998's Lifetime Achievement Award by the Academy of Television Arts and Sciences. Preceded by a tribute from Maya Angelou, an emotional Winfrey was presented with the award by Barbara Walters. "To be able to use this tremendous vehicle of television to go into people's homes and somehow be able to touch their lives, to be the beacon that Barbara [Walters] was for me, to be a light of hope and understanding . . . is the greatest blessing

God could have given me," Winfrey told the crowd at Radio City Music Hall. "And I want to continue to use television . . . to make people lead better lives, to lead them to the highest vision possible for themselves."[8]

If Winfrey's plans for the future are any indication, she will continue to do just that.

The year 2011 marks the debut of OWN: The Oprah Winfrey Network, which is projected to reach approximately 80 million homes. Taking over what was

A fan holds a copy of the *Chicago Sun-Times* featuring Oprah Winfrey on the front page. During the November 20, 2009, broadcast of *The Oprah Winfrey Show*, Winfrey announced that the program will air for the last time on September 9, 2011, after a twenty-five-year run.

formerly the Discovery Health Channel, OWN will offer programming in Winfrey's areas of interest: self-help, lifestyle, spirituality, and entertainment. "We'll deal with topics such as money, health and relationships. I want to create . . . a place where people can go to feel better about their lives," Winfrey said during a press conference.[9] For Winfrey, the opportunity is her second chance to create a cable network; in 1998, she had been one of the primary investors in Oxygen but later sold her shares because the network's direction "didn't reflect [her] voice."[10]

Along with OWN, Winfrey's small-screen efforts will continue to expand in light of the partnership between Harpo Films and HBO. In late 2008, Winfrey announced a three-year deal between the two entities enabling her to create movies, documentaries, and miniseries for the popular cable network. Harpo has also experienced continued success in the feature film arena; its most recent movie, *The Great Debaters*, earned several NAACP Image Awards and a Golden Globe nomination. Starring Denzel Washington, the film is based a true story and explores racial tensions in the 1930s.

As for *The Oprah Winfrey Show,* the show will cease production and conclude its syndication run in 2011, which will be its twenty-fifth anniversary on the air. "This show has been my life, and I love it enough to know when it's time to say goodbye," Winfrey told viewers in an emotional announcement in November 2009. "Twenty-

Winfrey addresses graduates at the Stanford University commencement ceremony in Palo Alto, California, June 15, 2008.

five years feels right in my bones and it feels right in my spirit. It's the perfect number—the exact right time. So I hope that you will take this 18-month ride with me right through to the final show."[11]

Many speculate that her talk show will continue in a different format on OWN: The Oprah Winfrey Network. In the meantime, her show continues to be a pioneer in its field. In 2008, *Oprah* became one of the first daytime talk shows to broadcast in high-definition. Filmed in Chicago's Millennium Park, the hi-def season premiere spotlighted

Olympic gold medalists such as Michael Phelps and Misty May-Treanor.

Winfrey's protégés, such as Dr. Phil and Rachael Ray, also continue their success in syndication. Dr. Phil maintains the #2 spot in ratings (behind Oprah), while Ray took home the 2008 and 2009 Daytime Emmys for Outstanding Talk Show—Entertainment. And history may soon be looking to repeat itself: another spin-off show featuring Dr. Mehmet Oz debuted in September 2009 to high ratings.[12] On the show, Dr. Oz discusses medical and health hot topics, as well as how to become a "more magnificent you." Next up for a TV show is design expert Nate Berkus, whose premiere is planned for September 2010.[13] Also, actress Jenny McCarthy has signed a development deal with Winfrey that includes an Internet blog, appearances on *Oprah*, and possibly a talk show.[14]

It is clear Winfrey has no problem sharing her success— and why not? After all, there is plenty to go around! In a 2005 Greatest American poll, Winfrey was the only woman to land a top-ten spot alongside such historical greats as Martin Luther King, Jr., Ronald Reagan, Abraham Lincoln, and Benjamin Franklin. (And the media appears to agree: *Time* magazine named Winfrey one of its "Most Important Americans of the 20th Century" in 1999, and *Newsweek* named her its "Woman of the New Century.")[15]

Yet beneath all the superlatives lies an "everywoman" who lives the same highs and lows as the women whose television sets she appears on each day. From her weight fluctuations to her abused past to her relationships, Winfrey has always been open about her personal struggles. For that reason, Winfrey is credited (and at times criticized) for creating our society's "confessional" culture. Once-taboo topics are now openly discussed on national television. Audience members linger after Winfrey's tapings to share their own experiences on the day's topic, with "After the Show" footage often rolling on Oprah.com. "My ability to get people to open up is only attributed, I think, to the fact that there is a common bond in the human spirit," Winfrey has said. "We all want the same things. And I know that. I really do know that I am no different than anybody else."[16]

This "life as open book" approach speaks to Winfrey's most ardent wish for both herself and humanity: to embrace their authentic selves (or, as merchandise for sale at the Oprah Store proclaims, "Become more of yourself"). Her quest for personal truth has inspired many to look inward for answers and to strive for self-acceptance. And not only has Winfrey shared herself with her audience, she has also shared her considerable fortune with the world in the name of doing good—making her the ultimate celebrity with heart. "There's no better way to make your mark on the world and to share that abundance with others," Winfrey said in a Stanford University graduation address. "My constant prayer for myself is to be used in service for the greater good."[17]

Chronology

1954—Oprah Gail Winfrey is born on January 29 to Vernita Lee and Vernon Winfrey.

1959—Young Oprah starts kindergarten but is more advanced than the other students and promptly moves to first grade.

1967—Oprah receives a scholarship to Milwaukee's Nicolet High School.

1986—*The Oprah Winfrey Show* hits airwaves.

1988—Winfrey becomes the youngest person ever to receive the International Radio and Television Society's Broadcaster of the Year Award; Winfrey pulls a red wagon carrying sixty-seven pounds of fat on to the stage to symbolize her dramatic weight loss.

1989—In a partnership with restaurant guru Richard Melman, Winfrey opens The Eccentric restaurant in Chicago.

1994—Winfrey runs the Washington, D.C., Marine Corps Marathon.

1998—Winfrey appears on the cover of *Vogue*; Winfrey cofounds Oxygen Media, an Internet business and cable network.

1999—Winfrey and Stedman Graham co-teach a course titled "The Dynamics of Leadership" at Northwestern University in Chicago.

2002— Winfrey receives an honorary doctorate degree in fine arts from Princeton University.

2004—Tom Cruise and Winfrey cohost the Nobel Peace Prize concert in Oslo, Norway, featuring stars such as Patti LaBelle and Cyndi Lauper.

2005—A musical production of *The Color Purple* debuts on Broadway, produced and financially backed by Winfrey; Oprah's Angel Network provides more than $1 million in school supplies to eighteen thousand South African children in need.

2006—Winfrey appears on the PBS program *African-American Lives* for a DNA test that determines she is 89 percent Sub-Saharan African, 8 percent American Indian, and 3 percent East Asian.

2007—Winfrey breaks her previous political silence to publicly endorse Democratic candidate Barack Obama for president.

2008—The Oprah Store opens across the street from Harpo Studios, with many of the proceeds supporting Oprah's Angel Network; Winfrey announces the launch of the Oprah Winfrey Network (OWN) for 2011.

2009—Winfrey announces that *The Oprah Winfrey Show* will end its run in 2011, its twenty-fifth anniversary.

Selected Awards

1986—Woman of Achievement Award, National Organization for Women

1989—Entertainer of the Year, NAACP Image Awards

1990—America's Hope Award

1993—Horatio Alger Award

1996—George Foster Peabody Award

Television Academy Hall of Fame Induction

1998—Lifetime Achievement Award, National Academy of Television Arts and Sciences

1999—50th Anniversary Gold Medal Award, National Book Foundation

2002—Bob Hope Humanitarian Award, National Academy of Television Arts and Sciences

2003—Honors Award, Association of American Publishers

Marian Anderson Award

2004—Candle for Lifetime Achievement in Humanitarian Service Award, Morehouse College

Global Leadership Award, United Nations Association

2005—Hall of Fame Inductee, NAACP Image Awards

2007—Elie Wiesel Foundation Humanitarian Award

2008—Person of the Year, PETA (People for the Ethical Treatment of Animals)